REFLECTIONS
OF
GLOSSOP

Margaret Buxton - Knott

Authors note

As the daughter of a well known local photographer (the late Harry Buxton), I have used numerous examples of his work and collection to compile this book in an attempt to record something of the interesting historical and topical moments in the life of Glossop, Derbyshire. If the reader has lived through or even experienced some of these moments, I hope the illustrations will revive a feeling of nostalgia and memories of some of the perhaps more happier times. For those too young to remember, I hope this look at the past will help you to appreciate how Glossop has both evolved and changed over the years.

Margaret Buxton - Knott

Copyright© 1995 Foxline Publishing and Margaret Knott
ISBN 1 870119 37 1
All rights reserved
Designed and Edited by Gregory K. Fox
Typeset by Bill Rear, Johnstown, Wrexham
Printed by the Amadeus Press, Huddersfield

Published by Foxline publishing
32, Urwick Road, Romiley, Stockport SK6 3JS

Acknowledgement
My thanks to Peggy and Derek at Glossop Heritage Centre for their help in gathering the information required to write the stories behind the photographs.

Introduction

The Manor of Glossop in Derbyshire came to the Howards in 1606 when Alathea Talbot married the 14th Earl of Arundel, Thomas Howard. Glossop became a Municipal Borough in 1866 when the Charter arrived at Glossop railway station.
Glossopdale had ten townships although only seven came within the new borough - Charlesworth, Chisworth, Ludworth, Whitfield,Glossop, Padfield and Hadfield. It had three wards - All Saints,St. James, and Hadfield.The five towns of Glossop were accepted to be Milltown (the area round the Corn Mill), Freetown (named after the the freeholders who lived in the area), Leantown (named during times of hardship), Jerrytown (named after Jerry Sykes who built houses along High Street West in the 1800's) and Roughtown (part of Old Glossop near Hope Street).In the Domesday survey, Glossop was spelt Glosop; Dinting was Dentic, and Whitfield was Witfield.

Dedication

I dedicate this book to all who have lived in Glossop, especially to the memory of my late father, Harry Buxton (1908 - 1983).As one of his former work colleagues once said, "He was the photographer of the unexpected and never left home without a camera". He took and processed his first photograph when he was only seven years of age. During the war he served as a police photographer in Glossop. He was a member of Glossop Borough Council in the early 1970's and gave many photographic slide lectures to local societies. He also had a great interest in amateur and CB radio.

Other titles by the same author.

"Hattersley - The old and the new"
ISBN 1-870119-31-2   Price £4-95

Other Foxline titles about Glossop. For details of price and availability, contact your local bookseller or send a stamped addressed envelope to :-
Foxline Publishing, 32 Urwick Road, Romiley, Stockport,Cheshire. SK6 3JS

Town Hall. c. 1860. Built in 1838 by Bernard Edward Howard (12th Duke of Norfolk and Lord of the Manor), shops were incorporated into the building - the Consumers Tea Company can be seen on the right. The Market Hall was built in 1844 (centre arch). To the right is the Pawnbroker and General Clothier. Before 1838 the administrative centre for the town was in Old Glossop, near the Cross. It was in 1860 that some main roads aquired gas street lighting.

Norfolk Square, May 1902. At the end of the Boer War (which started in October 1899) the Boers agreed to be subjects of King Edward V11 and peace celebrations were held.

The sign on the Henry Street building says, '*By the help of our God and our Noble Men we celebrate victory and Joy with thanksgiving*'.

Horses had been collected from Glossop farmers earlier in the war at this same spot for the war. In July 1902 an Ox-Roasting took place on the Market Ground to celebrate the Coronation of King Edward V11.

Glossop Officials walking down Norfolk Street, after the churching of the Mayor in the 1890's. Front - Doctor MacKenzie and R. Dickenson. Centre - S. Fletcher and J. Walkden. Back - William Shepley Rhodes (mayor 1891 - 1892) and Herbert Rhodes (mayor 1895 - 1896). Far left - S. Dane. The Rhodes family lived at Mersey Bank House in Hadfield.

1905 Horse Parade.
Horse parade passing Norfolk Square. The first vehicle was a fire engine pulled by four horses. The inscription on the second cart says, '*Success to the Horse Parade*'. The drinking fountain on the right was given by Mrs. Wood in 1881. Notice the gas street lamps and cobbled sets.

(Above). **Mayor Thomas Braddock,** 1905, the 19th Glossop Mayor. The first was Francis Sumner in 1866 and the last was George Chatterton in 1973.

(left) The war memorial was erected in Norfolk Square in 1920 to remember the dead in the First World War (1914 - 1918).

1910 the Mayor, Ald. Brook Furniss reads the proclaimation of assention to the throne of King George V and Queen Mary, to the towns folk of Old Glossop. Oswald Partington and Edward Partington, who became Lord Doverdale in 1912, were in the crowd.

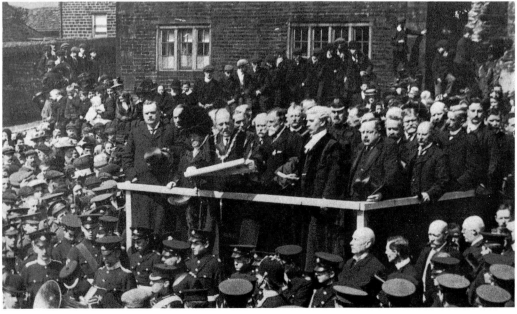

High Street East in 1914. The crowds were waiting for the Mayoral procession to Old Glossop Church. Herbert Partington was the Mayor from 1913 - 1915. The tram in the distance would be on its way to the Queen's Arms near Manor Park.

Dinting Viaduct, was built in 1844 with five laminated wooden arches separating the masonry approach spans. This orginated the name of *Dinting Arches*, a title still locally applied. Replacement of these arches took place within twenty years when the deep wrought iron girders of which we are familiar were installed. The symmetry of the bridge was severely affected by the strengthening work of 1918-19 when seven brick piers were built. This view from the Glossop side of the arches shows the viaduct before the days of the additional piers.

Whitfield Well Dressing, c.1920. Miss McKilroy is standing on the cart, the two men either side are Mr. Williams and Mr. Aveson. The annual 'Wild Weekend' included a fair and the rush cart as well as bands playing for dancing, climbing the greasy pole, coconut shies and the blessing of the local wells. In 1927 these wells still served a large number of houses in the Whitfield area.

1920's

Tree planting at Simmondley in the 1920's. It was near here that Albert Edward Burrows deposited the bodies of his son Albert, lover Hannah Calladine and her son and daughter down the Simmondley Pits in 1923. He was hung at Nottinghamshire later that year for their murder.

(right). 1927. Richard Sellars and his daughter, Ivy presenting the prizes at the Grammer School's sports day.

(left). Mrs. Sutherland of York Street with her talking budgie in the thirties.

1927

(below). **Glossop Football Club 1927 - 1928.** Samuel Hill Wood played on the wing from 1890 and used his influence to gain the North End club a place in the second division. He spent over £10,000 financing the club. Here is the team seen with the Manchester League Cup, which they won in 1927 - 1928 season. They were the winners of the Gilgryst Cup in 1922/3, 1929/30, 1934/5 and 1948/49.

Longden's Corner, 1931.
Longden's corner got its name from the farm which stood at the junction of Woodhead Road and Cemetery Road. The tenant farmer at that time was Alfred Longden. Children from Shrewsbury Street Methodist Chapel went on field days to Blackshaw Farm on Woodhead Road. The older ones walked and the young ones were taken by lorry to enjoy games, races and current cakes. The car is a Baby Austin Seven and was my father's first car. It cost £130 when new in 1930.

New Fire Engine, c. 1935.
Alderman Robert Beckman named Glossop's new fire engine after his daughter, Beatrice, outside the Town Hall. The Fire Station was on Ellison Street. Earlier in this book (page 4) you will have seen a horse - drawn vehicle in 1905.

May 1936. At the Cross in Old Glossop, Councillor John Hague and his party pose for this photograph, after the Mayor Making Ceremony. It was at this place that all ceremonial and traditional activity took place. Weekly markets were held here from 1289 - 1833. The cap was added to the top of the Cross shaft in 1910, and the whole structure was moved away from the house to a more central position in the square.

Manor Park, c. 1936. A Newton Jazz Band at the carnival in the park. The grounds of the old Glossop Hall were opened in 1927 as Manor Park. At the official opening there was a rose queen pageant, decorated horses, bands, fancy dress, tradesmen's lorries, Morris Dancers, Guides and Scouts. The entrance fee was one shilling and six pence for children. For two shillings and six pence an immunity badge from collections could be bought in advance.

1936. Cotton Queen Doris Bower from Bolton, is greeted by Mayor Hague at the door of 'Bon Marche' in Glossop. The queens were chosen from different districts in the cotton mills of the North. The first queen was Francess Lockett from Glossop in 1930. In 1938 the prize money for winning was £50.

December 14th 1936. The Abdication of King Edward V111 read by John Hague from the Town Hall steps. The King was never crowned and had acceded the throne in January 1936. He chose to marry Mrs. Simpson and was succeeded by George V1 and Queen Elizabeth on 10th December 1936 and they were crowned 12th May 1937.

May 7th 1937. Norfolk Square decorated for the Coronation Of King George VI and Queen Elizabeth. The flag was raised on the Town Hall and bunting displayed on other memorable occasions. One of these being on Armistice day (November 11th 1918), later in the following year a celebration of peace was held in the square, when choirs from local churches and chapels sang.

1937

May 12th 1937. Celebrations for the Coronation of King George VI and Queen Elizabeth at Bernard Street and Edward Street, off Arundel Street. Under the garland arch, on the left, huge ladders were used to put up the last of the decorations. A poster aptly displays the sentiments of the age, '*God Save The King*'.

Bernard Street This close-up shows John Hague, Richard Sellars and other officials viewing the tableau of the royal coach and horses. The chimneys of Sumner's Mill can be seen through the lines of bunting on the left of the picture.

May 1937. One of the King's first duties was the sending off a telegram to Mrs. Hannah Cresswell Kenyon on the occasion of her hundreth birthday. She died a few weeks later.

July 1937. Hawley's Dome on the corner of Victoria Street being demolished. The Newsagent and bookseller's moved to 6. High Street East. It was replaced by Burton's the tailor's, and later became the Midland Bank. Much earlier a Barber's shop occupied this site and it was then known as Bradbury's Corner

Meadow Mills, 1937. These sixteen cottages next to Meadow Mills stood at the top of Shepley Street. The area known as the Wharf is on the way to Mossy Lea. Behind the cottages were two lodges, of which the higher one supplied water to drive the machinery in the cotton mill by water wheel. The cottages were demolished in October 1964.

October 1937. At this time the fire brigade was on Ellison Street, next to the police station. All fire-fighting vehicles, including those once drawn by horses, were housed here. In May 1972 the fire service transferred to Charlestown Road, near Whitfield House. The picture shows the fire engine that pumped water from Gamesley reservoir to Town Lane reservoir in Charlesworth, a distance of 1200 yards and 150 feet higher.

Tree planting, May 1937. Commemorative Oak saplings were planted in local parks to celebrate the coronation. The oak was chosen to typify the steadfastness and sturdiness of the British character. Deputy Mayor, Counc. Beckman is seen planting a tree in Manor Park. He was made a Freeman of Glossop in 1962 aged 72. Other officials present were, Alderman Platt, Mayor John Hague, Mayoress Mrs. Oulton, G. Wharmby, J. Buckley, R. Sellars, Pastor Gaunt (Mayor's Chaplain) and R. Green-Smith (Chief Constable).

September 1937. This lorry was carrying a new pipe organ for the church at Whitfield. It had travelled from Messrs. Abbot & Smith's works at Leeds when it crashed on a bend on the Holme Moss Road near Woodhead. The church had hoped that it would have been installed and fully working by October, but due to such severe damage this was impossible.

Young workers from Wood's Mill, c. 1938. The girls seem to be representing the various jobs in the weaving shed - Carding, Spinning, Winding - The girl on the right is showing the traditional mill clothing of clogs and shawl.

July 1938. The British Legion 8th. Drumhead Service in Manor Park. The procession of ex - servicemen started from the market ground and was led by Glossop Military band. The service was led by Rev. A. C. M. White from St. Andrew's church in Hadfield.

1938/39

January 1939. Mrs. Torkington at the Arundel Arms near Glossop Cemetery, known locally as the "Deadmans". It was the headquarters for Glossop Farmer's cricket club. In winter it was frequently cut off because of bad weather. In 1946 it was isolated for seven weeks due to the deep snow. Some of the landlords were Arthur Roe, Jim Hadfield, George Lewis, Lloyd Jackson, Arthur George Currums and Harry Torkington. Here Mrs. Torkington is cleaning over 100 pieces of brass and copper that decorated the public bar. The display was used to raise cash for local charities. In the 'fifties the former pub opened as a boarding kennel. Also, local coach and taxi firms rented space to site transmitter aerials.

May 1939 saw the opening of the recruitment centre in Victoria Street by the Mayor, Alderman Richard Sellars. 250 men were seen by twelve members of the British Legion. The men came to enlist into the Royal Signal Corp. and the Derbyshire Territorial Army Association. Compulsory National Service (Conscription) for all males reaching the age of twenty, happened in peace time until 1960.

1939

The Snake Inn, c. 1939. The family of Longden were tenants until 1879. In 1939 the licensee, Isaac Rowarth built the new wing. The inn is situated 1086 feet above sea level on the Snake Road (A57) near Ashopton , and is the most remote inn in Derbyshire. In 1818 Parliament gave the go-ahead to a trade route over the Snake Pass. Previously the trade-route between Manchester and Sheffield had been via Castleton. Thomas Telford was the engineer for the new road. It was opened in 1821 and at the time, was one of the highest turnpike roads in England, reaching a height of 1680' The Snake Inn had been built at the top of Woodlands Valley just before the opening of the road. At first it was named Lady Clough, after the clough nearby, but as a mark of respect to the Duke of Devonshire, it was renamed the Snake Inn, part of the Devonshire crest being a snake. The first landlord was John Longden, a methodist preacher, who held prayer meetings at the inn. In the field opposite, prize fights were held. In the photograph the bus from Glossop is heading for Ashopton and Sheffield. A horse is stabled in the building to the left. The building on the extreme left was occupied by the game keeper.

May 1939. Margaret Pearson crowns Mary (Our Lady) at St Mary's church. The church was built in 1887 in memory of Francis Sumner, a local millowner who had died in 1884. Pope Leo X111 laid the foundation stone in July 1886. The parish priest of All Saints in Old Glossop, Father Theodore Fauvel had a lot to do with establishing the new church. In May 1987 the church held celebrations to mark the centenary. The odd numbered houses on Sumner Street were built from the stone left over from the church.

1939. The last rush cart at Whitfield outside the Roebuck Inn. The landlord Mr. Broadley was one of the men pictured here. The annual 'Wild Weekend' included Rush Bearing and the Fair. Rushes were carried on the cart to spread on the floors of churches before carpets.

In 1939 rain caused severe flooding, as it has on many occasions in the town. Above is the remains of Dinting Vale Bridge over Glossop Brook, the road that leads to Dinting Road via the level crossing. In 1994 work started on sections of the Brook, by the National Rivers Authority, to prevent flooding in the future. At Mossy Lea in Old Glossop, stepped rocks have provided mini - waterfalls to prevent silt from being washed downstream. At the bridge near Tesco, on High Street West, a five feet build up of silt will be dug out and similar work will take place at Dinting near Glossop Caravans. Below is the scene on Flag Fields, below Turn Lee paper mill, after the flooding of Gnat Holle Brook in 1939.

Model Farm, off Woodhead Road in the 1930's. Also known as Laneside Farm, it was built by Lord Howard. The woodland behind is Cat Wood and was planted in 1894. Harry Buxton can be seen in the foreground talking to two friends.

June 1939. Opening of the temporary headquarters for the Territorial Army by Alderman Sellars. The parade of 1st and 2nd companies of the 2nd North Midland Corps. of Signals was on land between Dinting Church and the viaduct

September 1939. Glossop Territorial Army volunteers were cheered by large crowds as they marched through the town before going to camp at Skegness. The Mayor took the salute in Norfolk Square. On their return, large crowds again welcomed them back. Glossop Old Band led the procession seen here near the railway station in Norfolk Street. Notice the small boy who perhaps wished he was old enough to join, on the left of the picture. The Second World War was declared on September 3rd 1939.

In preperation for war, The local Territorials set off for camp at Skegness in 1939. They are seen here at the corner of High Street and Victoria Street. The shops on the corner include, The North Western Road Car Company, Robinson & Wood and an advertisement for Brownsons Tailors.

Glossop Cemetery, c.1939. In 1857 a Burial Board was formed and as a result, six acres of land was bought at Allman's Heath to supplement the overflowing local chuchyards. Next to the cemetery the Arundel Arms stood, because of its location it became known as the Deadman's Arms. A legend went round that if a pint of ale was left on the cemetery wall, an unseen body would drink it.

1939/40

The Town Hall, c.1940, Bernard Edward Howard, the 12th Duke of Norfolk and Lord of the Manor, had built the Town Hall in 1838 when the local council moved its administrative centre from Old Glossop. The pillars were constucted c. 1925 with the idea of building a wall around, but these were removed in 1950. On the pillar a sign read, *NO THROUGH ROAD FOR VEHICLES OVER THE MARKET GROUND.* The Municipal building was altered in the early 1920's. In the centre of the building on the extreme left, was the entrance to the old fish market. In 1911 the entrance to the general market was made here.

(Below). **September 1940. Alderman Richard (Dick) Sellars got a civic send off,** when at the age of 70, he set off with a Barrel Organ to raise money for the Spitfire Fund. Lord Beaverbrook, The Minister of Aircraft Production during the war, set up this fund in1940 to encourage donations for specific wartime equipment. The deputy Mayoress, Miss Ivy Sellars accompanied her father on the tour around the borough. There were many helpers to push and turn the barrel organ. His visits included Charlesworth and Chisworth and a tremendous reception was given everywhere. One letter received said, *Good Old Dick, carry on the good work.* The Mayor at the time was Joseph Taylor and Councillor Roberts was amongst the officials. Alderman Sellars was very well turned out in his shining Topper, white spats, well cut Frock Coat and smartly creased trousers. Mr. Hugh Molson, The Derbyshire M. P. sent £25, a total of £208 being raised by the end of the week. Mr. Sellars also organised a football match between local butchers and licensed victuallers to raise more cash for the fund.

June 1940. Evacuees arrived in Glossop by Train, they came from Lowestoft. Mr C. Lord was the Chief Billeting Officer. The Carriage Company & North Western Road Car Company laid on buses to take some children to Hadfield, some to the Victoria Hall and the rest to the Market Hall. The children were sent to live with local families. Many of their fathers were local fishermen who later helped to bring home the British Expeditionary Force from Flanders. They were the British Army who served in France.

At this time regular gas drills were held in schools and work places. At a given signal, everyone had to put on a gas mask as quickly as possible. Children soon learnt that they could blow 'raspberries' through their masks. They were red and black to resemble Mickey Mouse and special masks were made to completely enclose babies. Volcrepe factory produced 6,000 gas masks for horses and mules and 48 million earphone pads for service radio equipment during war time.

May 1941, War Weapons Week. More money for for the war effort was encouraged to be saved during the special week. The idea was to raise enough for a flight of five Bombers. This £100,000 indicator, erected in Norfolk Square said, "Make £200,000 and bump 'em off". It referred to Hitler and Mussolini, the two dictators of Europe. By June £233,022 had been raised by local firms and churches.

All the money accumulated in the War Weapons Week (May 24th - 31st 1941) was turned into War Bonds. A telegram from the Chancellor of the Exchequer was sent to the Mayor congratulating Glossop's War effort. By 1945 a tank named 'Glossop" and a submarine had been bought from the Bonds. Other savings schemes that followed were - Warships 1942, Wings of Victory 1943, Salute the Soldier 1944, Defence Bonds, Post Office Savings and National Savings.

November 1941. A gathering of Civil Defence Personnel from Glossop and surrounding areas on the Market Ground, next to the Town Hall. It was an Auxillary Fire Service exercise to see how quickly support could be bought into Glossop to deal with imaginary fires started by an enemy blitz. Men were called out from Manchester, Liverpool and the Midlands. Fifty motor drawn trailer pumps, one hundred motor vehicles, dispatch riders, mobile canteens and about three hundred firemen gathered. The reinforcements were allocated various fire points and had to tackle imaginary fires. This was the way the Home Front was prepared to win the war.

1941

1941 Councillor Haigh of Lambgates, Hadfield, reviews the Special Constables on the Market Ground. The Specials were volunteers who gave up some of their time to support the regular constables. Many were enrolled in 1926, at the time of the General Strike to maintain essential services. The Special Constables' Act of 1831 officially gave Chief Police Officers the power to appoint Specials

1941/42

William Barstow, who was a sergeant in Glossop Borough Police Force. He was an instructor to A. R. P. Special Constable. In 1944 he joined the A. M. G. O. T. (Allied Military Government Of Occupied Territory) as Lieutenant.

(Opposite-right). **1942 Police Station, Ellison Street.** During the 2nd World War volunteers answered the call to serve on the Home Front as Special Constables, as many of the regular young officers had enlisted into the forces. The Police Act of 1839 had brought an allocation of professional, uniformed County Policemen to Glossop. There should have been one officer to every 3,000 poulation, therefore six should have come, but Glossop got only two. In the picture is my Father, Police War Reservist Harry Buxton, who acted as the force photographer from 1941 - 1945 during the war. During the 1st World War, a full uniform with a peaked cap was worn by all Special Constables and when off duty, an enamel lapel badge was authorised to be worn on civilian clothing. Additionally, many wore a badge inscribed *On War Duty,* issued to those in reserved occupations, to prevent a "misguided" public expression of patriotic fervour, and who might present a "white feather" for cowardice, in the belief that they were conciencious objectors. By the commencement of the Second World War the public had accepted the Specials as a necessary force to fight the war at home.

25th June 1943. Explosion at Olive & Partington's Paper Mill, Charlestown Road. At the time of this disaster it was known as Turn Lee Paper Mill. A spherical boiling pan, twelve feet in diameter and weighing six tons, exploded in the Pan House of the Mill. Sulphur fumes were released and spread over the town. Four men, Moses Wrigley, Charles Newton, Tom Fielding and Frank Johnson, died with many other workers badly scalded.

1943

Partington's Paper Mill - the Pan House before the disaster

Steam 'Tiger" tractors were used to haul logs and other goods from the railway station to Olive & Partington's Mill. After the explosion in 1943 these traction engines and lorries were used to clear the debris. In 1990 a Glossop Tiger Tractor restored by David Cope of Cromford, was brought to the Victorian Weekend in the town.

1940's

An 'Iron Monster' outside the Drover's Arms on Turn Lee Road. From 1914 steam traction engines were owned by Glossop Haulage. These trucks are covered with tarpaulin bearing the name 'John Walton, Glossop, Derbyshire'. Walton's had a Bleach Works at Charlestown from 1869 until they moved to Hollingworth in 1952.

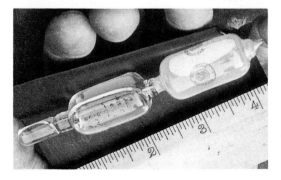

(Right) An Incendiary Bomb that fell near Glossop but never ignited.

(Left). The detonator from the bomb that dropped near the Snake Pass in 1943.

Melandra Railway Bridge, Brookfield. The scene of many floods over the years. It was a common sight to see sand bags at the doors of the terraced houses along this road.

1944

May 1944. The worst flood on record happened in 1944. The damage was estimated at £200,000. The storm started at 4.30pm with large hailstones, thunder and lightning and by 7.30pm 6.52 inches of rain had fallen, At the Junction Inn (above) where the Gnat Hole Brook joins the Glossop Brook at Bray Clough water from the swollen brooks spilled over the road and four to five feet of water swept into the bar up to the shelves of bottles forcing the landlady Mrs. Demain and her daughter to flee up the stairs. In Old Glossop between Hope Street and Wesley Street the flood water broke the stone parapet of the bridge, littering the road with masonary. Water crashed through the doors of the Wesley Chapel. The area near the Old Cross became a swirling pool. Mr. Hinchliffe, the landlord of the Queen's Arms served, in waders and the barrels in the cellar were afloat and banging on the ceiling. In Brookfield nearly all the houses were flooded as water from Woolley Bridge and Dinting created a huge pond in the fields beyond the filter beds and across the road. In part of Dinting Printworks the water burst through a 150 ton pile of coal and coke and through a wall, carrying coal, bricks and stone into the back yards of houses as the bottom of Shaw Lane. Two men from Dinting Lodge cottages went to rescue pigs belonging to Dinting Printworks Pig Club. All were led to safety. The wife of one of the men decided to climb out of an upstairs window to reach a neighbour, but fell through a skylight, cutting her legs badly and narrowly escaping falling into the water below.

Mrs. Jane Ann Bridge of George Street had been viewing the damage caused by the flood with her sister-in-law Sarah Ann Johnson when the iron bridge collapsed, sweeping her away in the raging water. Her body was found in the river Etherow some days later near Marple.

The storm caused the Reservoir to overflow at the Bleachworks in Charlestown Road. Pieces of machinery were washed out onto the road with bales of wood pulp floating about at Turn Lee Paper Mill. The brook known locally at the time as the "Chemic", washed away hundreds of tons of logs from the wood pile. These came downstream to Dinting like lumber over the Canadian rapids. It was carried into Dinting Vale, where terrified residents could hear the logs hitting their doors. A dam of timber formed against the walls and railings of Holy Trinity Church and school, preventing much flooding of these buildings. (*Below*) The remainder of the logs lined the street and others were carried as far afield as Stockport, littering fields and gardens along the way.

Between 1930 and 1939, the years of the Depression, nearly three million were unemployed in Britain. Men with a wife and children received only £1.10s. 0d. (£1.50p) per week, and one quarter of the nation were under-nourished, ill clad and badly housed. Clothes became rationed in June 1941, and make-do-and-mend became the rule. Despite this, wartime brides scrimped and saved their coupons to make their big day as special as possible.

In October 1942 the Government banned real wedding cakes because of the shortage of food. Many couples improvised using cardboard shapes covered with chalk icing and when topped with some decoration no one was any the wiser, unless the knife went in too far!

In October 1945 Ada and Arthur Hodgkins married at the Elim church just as the R.A F. band was passing, leading a Thanksgiving Parade through the town. On seeing the couple, the band spontaneously formed a guard of honour, playing appropriately.

Wartime Weddings - Where are they now?

Many were married whilst the bridegroom was home on leave, but could only spend a short time together before a recall to duties.

Large bouquets and hats were very fashionable and for those that could manage it, a "wreath and veil" were the accepted order of the day. Many had to manage with their best dress or suit. In 1936 the Duchess of Kent had made eye-veils on hats a fashion item, and after the Coronation in 1937, powder blue, being the Queen's favourite colour, was copied by all who could afford new clothes.

From 1939 the Government began to deliver air-raid shelters around the country. People were advised to keep buckets of sand and a bath of water to extinguish any fires started by raids. Sandbags were piled high to protect important buildings and air-raid posts from bomb damage. Search-lights, using powerful arc-lamps, were used to scan the skies for enemy aircraft. These gave a brilliant light which was also very hot. A parabolic mirror was used to reflect the light rays in a parallel beam. It was mounted so the beam could be turned in any direction.

Dinting Vale before the electrification of the railway in 1954. Gas lamps lit the street. Holy Trinity Church and school are on the right. The Food Drink of the People seemed to be Bournville Cocoa.

During the war many women started to work as conductresses on the buses and continued for many years. Fine net was placed on the bus and train windows to prevent passengers being injured from flying glass during a raid.

Wartime

Women also worked in war factories to boost the output of much needed war materials. 75,000 girls joined the land army in Britain. Women also became ambulance drivers for the first time, whilst many joined Forces organisations such as the Women's Royal Naval Service, the Auxiliary Territorial Service and the Women's Auxiliary Air Force.

May 8th 1945, V. E. Day. Crowds gathered in Norfolk Square to hear the news that war in Europe had ended, resulting in the proclamation of a National holiday. Later there was dancing in the streets, with parties, fancy dress parades and the lighting of bonfires in celebration.

1944/45

During black out, no light was permitted to show. Outside, vehicle headlights had to be shaded and only a torch with two layers of tissue paper was permitted in the streets. People had been singing a popular wartime song, *When the Lights Come On Again* since 1942. In 1944 the black-out gave way to a half-hearted dim-out, and the Home Gaurd was stood down in November. Bonfires had been forbidden during the black-out years, and to celebrate peace many were lit. Usually they were built on high points such as Whiteley Nab and when set alight, were beacons to the towns below.

As the war came to an end Fancy Dress Parties were very popular. This group are on the steps of the Victoria Hall. The dress reflected war themes with R.A.F. and Army camps. The plaque to the left of the door says, *This stone was laid by H. Rhodes Esq. one of the donors of this building July 1887.* There is a similar stone plaque on the other side of the door bearing the name of the other benefactor, E. Partington. Herbert Rhodes' family founded Mersey Mills and Edward Partington was the owner of the paper making factory at Turn Lee.

June 1945. Glossop's ex-prisoners of war held a party at the Fitzalan Street School paying tribute to all who had contributed to the door-to-door penny appeal, which had raised £7697. 19s. 9d. up until April 1945. The money had provided Red Cross Food Parcels for prisoners of war from Glossop, who had been held in occupied territory in Europe.

August 1946. Melandra railway bridge near the Spring Tavern at Brookfield. 2.5 inches of rain, which fell in one day, caused the river to burst its bank and severe flooding was again seen in this area. The miniature geysers were water coming up from the sewers. The bridge was demolished in 1966.

September 1946. Again heavy rain causes flooding in the fields below Melandra. The loacal paper reported that it was the worst rain for over sixty years.

In 1946 this four roomed cottage in Hope Street, Old Glossop, was burnt out. The 86 year old resident, Sarah Wood, died in the blaze.

1946

November 1946. Grinding stones were made at Greenwood Quarry in Glossop and sent out to Copenhagen to assist in the making of pulp for news print. The foundation stone for Shire Hill Hospital was also made at this quarry.

There was more time and light to read and Glossop Library opened up an extension to house more books. The screen is between what is now the Junior and the Reference libraries. Members of staff and the local council can be seen at the opening ceremony.

(Above). **As life began to get back to normal after the war,** there was time again for relaxation. Here is Bill Green, a painter, at the Gentlemen's Club in Ellison Street.

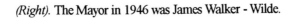

(Right). The Mayor in 1946 was James Walker - Wilde.

February 1947. The winter of 46 - 47 was one of the worst on record. Huge snow drifts up to bedroom windows isolated many families. This scene at Hawkshed in Old Glossop shows skiers making the most of it between walls of snow.

1947

July 1947. As the weather improved families took to the water, in the paddle boats in Manor Park, during the local Wakes holiday. The mills all closed down so that people could take a well earned break. Blackpool was a favourite place to go and special trains took many away from the local stations. Judging by the crowds on the banks, many enjoyed their holiday more locally.

December 1947. Five winners of a prize at Glossop's Film Ball went to Barton Aerodrome for a flight on this Avro plane 'The Mancunian'. They were Mr. & Mrs. Jack Holden, Mr. V. Rothwell, Miss J. Holt and Mr. R. Cherney.

1947

(Above). **November 1948. The Mayor Samuel Platt** congratulated Alderman Mellor on his 25 years service to the public.

Right: 1948 Stella Raddon, 19 year old Silver Lining Queen. Stella was crowned at the Empire cinema by film starlet Peggy Evans. The following day she unveiled a savings indicator in Norfolk Square to encourage private savings to aid production and improve conditions in the area. Mr. Hugh Molson M. P. was the main speaker of this savings campaign. The arrow on the indicator pointed to £200,000 when Stella unveiled it and it was hoped to reach the target of £300,000 by the end of Silver Lining Week. A dance to celebrate was held that night at Littlemoor School.

1949. Mary Clayton 69, of Hawthorne Cottage in Simmondley, had to spend most of her time in bed, due to sickness. She used her time to embroider and crochet.

1949

1949. John May had a basket making workshop in Victoria Street. His Father started the business in 1868 when he moved to Glossop. Mr. John May was a well known exponent of basket making, one of the world's oldest crafts, busy in his workshop.

Manor Park, c. 1949. It was opened to the public in 1927. It was given to Lord Howard of Glossop in 1616 by Gilber, Earl of Shrewsbury. This photograph shows the area that is now the rose garden.

1949

September 1949, Glossop Hall. It was announced that the Hall was to be sold to Kingsmoor School. It was the former residence of the Duke of Norfolk and was known as the Royal Hall in the 18th century. The school closed in July 1956 when it moved to the former St Andrews Junior School in Hadfield. The Hall was demolished in 1960 to make way for a housing estate.

1949, Wood's Baths in Howard Park. Mrs. Wood had this memorial built in front of the baths, to Daniel and Samuel Wood who died in 1888, and in memory of the town's dependence on cotton. Whiteley Nab can be seen in the distance.

(Left). **Local Alderman Richard (Dick) Sellars** who was then 77, was taken for a ride on the tree swing at the UNA (United Nations Association) garden party at the vicarage in Old Glossop. The UNA was formed in 1945 to promote peace and international cooperation and security. Mr. Sellars died in January 1956 aged 83 years.

1949. The author and her brother sample the delights of sweets as they came off ration. Food had been rationed from 1940. Petrol and sweets were rationed from 1942. Only 8 ounces of sweets or chocolate were allowed every 4 weeks provided coupons were saved. The demand for sweets was so great in 1949, that supplies ran out and had to be put back on ration until 4th February 1953.

1950. Amateur Radio Societies met around the country to try and contact enthusiasts in other parts. The Ashton, Glossop & District Radio Society were meeting here at the bottom of the Snake. My Father is on the extreme right. His call sign was G 2A JP. In retirement he turned to the hobby of C. B. radio, his call sign was then 'Matchstick Man' in memory of the painter L. S. Lowry who he'd met and photographed on many occasions.

1950

April 1950. Lunar eclipse seen at 9.55pm over Glossop. An eclipse of the moon can happen up to three times a year when the Earth passes between the Moon and the Sun. An eclipse of the Sun is when the Moon passes between it and the Earth. The next total eclipse of the Sun is expected in 1999. The ring around the Moon is made up of thin gases in the atmosphere.

May 1950. For many local children the annual trip to Belle Vue circus in Manchester was a highlight. Here, Robert Brothers travelling circus visited Glossop on Volcrepe sport's field. The boy with the clown was 9 year old David Wittington.

April 1950, Norfolk Arm[s]
Hotel. The licensee was Mr. E[
Smith. Around the back wer[e
stables where stage coache[s
once frequented. Outside wa[s
the then bus terminal. The
Hayfield, Chinley, Buxton No[
85 service is on the left. In
1964 it was proposed to pe[-
destrianise High Street West
from the Arundel Arms t[o
Norfolk Arms.

1950

1950, Market Ground. The
two pillars, built c. 1925, were
removed shortly after this
photograph was taken. They
had been built with the object
of building a wall around the
part of the Town Hall but as
this was never done, they no
longer served any purpose.
The No. 125 bus started from
here before the area became a
car park. The Bridge Inn, now
Dollars, and Shepley Mill, can
be seen in the distance.